629.224
SCH

WARDLAW ELEMENTARY SCHOOL
1698 Oakwood Ave.
Vallejo, CA 94591
(707) 556-8730

WITHDRAWN

Tractor Trailers

by Lola M. Schaefer

Consultant:
Larry Strawhorn
Vice President, Engineering
American Trucking Associations

Bridgestone Books
an imprint of Capstone Press
Mankato, Minnesota

Bridgestone Books are published by Capstone Press
151 Good Counsel Drive, P.O. Box 669, Mankato, Minnesota 56002
http://www.capstone-press.com

Copyright © 2000 Capstone Press. All rights reserved.
No part of this book may be reproduced without written permission from the publisher.
The publisher takes no responsibility for the use of any of the materials
or methods described in this book, nor for the products thereof.
Printed in the United States of America.

Library of Congress Cataloging-in-Publication Data
Schaefer, Lola M., 1950–
   Tractor Trailers/by Lola M. Schaefer.
   p. cm.—(The transportation library)
   Includes bibliographical references and index.
   Summary: Describes a tractor trailer and explains how it works and is used; includes a
brief history and facts about this form of transportation.
   ISBN 0-7368-0504-4
   1. Tractor trailer combinations—Juvenile literature. [1. Tractor trailers. 2. Trucks] I. Title.
II. Series.
TL230.15.S33 2000
629.224—dc21   99-053791
                                                                                                                    CIP

Editorial Credits
Karen L. Daas, editor; Timothy Halldin, cover designer and illustrator;
  Sara A. Sinnard, illustrator; Kimberly Danger, photo researcher

Photo Credits
Archive Photos, 14, 16–17
David R. Frazier Photolibrary, 4, 20
Highway Images/Bette S. Garber, 12, 18
Jack Glisson, 6–7
Photri-Microstock/Bill Barley, cover
Unicorn Stock Photos, 8

1 2 3 4 5 6 05 04 03 02 01 00

Table of Contents

Tractor Trailers

Tractor trailers are large trucks. They transport cargo from one place to another. They sometimes carry large, heavy loads. Tractor trailers have two main parts. The trailer holds the cargo. The tractor pulls the trailer.

transport

to move people and goods from one place to another

hood

exhaust pipes

fuel tank

fifth wheel

tire

The driver sits in the cab.
The engine is under the
hood. A fuel tank is on one
or both sides of the cab.
Hot gases from the engine
called exhaust come out
of exhaust pipes. A metal
plate on the back of the
tractor is called the fifth
wheel. A tractor has six
to ten tires.

landing gear

Parts of a Trailer

A trailer has a kingpin and landing gear. The kingpin works with the fifth wheel to lock the trailer to the tractor. Landing gear supports the front of the trailer when it is not locked to the tractor. Trailers have four to eight tires.

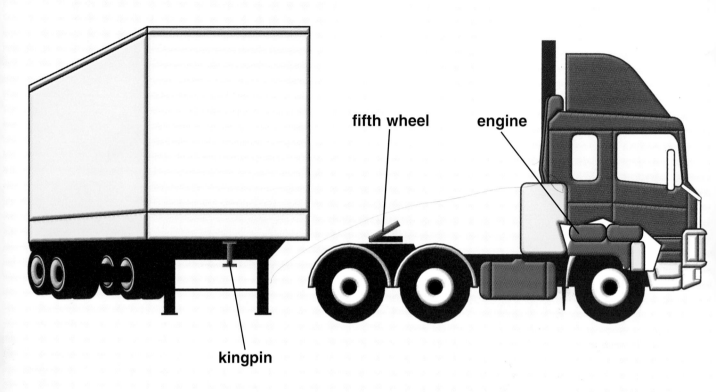

fifth wheel

engine

kingpin

How a Tractor Trailer Works

The driver attaches the tractor to a trailer. The tractor has a large diesel engine. Diesel fuel powers the engine. Power from the engine turns the tractor's tires. The tractor pulls the trailer.

diesel fuel

a heavy fuel that burns to make power

Driving a Tractor Trailer

Drivers sit in a tractor cab. They use a steering wheel, pedals, and levers to drive the tractor. Drivers pick up cargo at a loading dock and transport it to another place. They keep a log of time and distance travelled.

log
a written record

Before Tractor Trailers

People used trucks and trains to transport cargo before tractor trailers were invented. Trucks could not carry large, heavy loads. Trains could only deliver cargo to train stops.

Early Tractor Trailers

The earliest tractor trailers were trucks and wagons. People attached wagons to the back of trucks. These tractor trailers could not carry much cargo. Some tractors did not have cabs. The driver sat on a seat above a small fuel tank.

Tractor Trailers Today

Tractor trailers move many kinds of cargo. They carry items such as books and clothing. Refrigerated tractor trailers carry fresh food or flowers. Livestock trailers transport animals. Tank trailers hold liquids. Flatbed trailers carry large, heavy machinery.

Tractor Trailer Facts

- Some tractor trailers have more than one trailer. A second trailer can be joined to the back of the first trailer.

- Tractor trailers in the United States carry nearly 7 billion tons (6 metric tons) of cargo each year.

- A full tanker trailer holds more liquid than 200 bathtubs can hold.

- The fuel tanks on some tractors can hold almost 300 gallons (1,100 liters) of fuel.

- People attend driving schools to become tractor trailer drivers. Students train for 8 to 12 weeks. They study and practice driving for about 500 hours.

Hands On: Momentum

Tractor trailers take longer to stop than cars because tractor trailers have more momentum. Momentum is the force an object has when it is moving. All moving objects have momentum.

What You Need

A ruler
A quarter
A dime

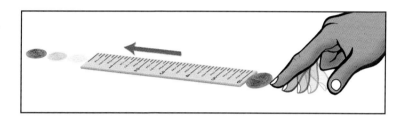

What You Do

1. Place the ruler flat on a table.
2. Place the dime on the table so that it touches one end of the ruler.
3. Flick the quarter at the other end of the ruler. The dime will move.
4. Place the quarter so that it touches one end of the ruler.
5. Flick the dime at the other end of the ruler. The quarter will move. But the quarter moves less than the dime moved.

The moving coin has momentum. The momentum is transferred through the ruler to the second coin. This momentum moves the second coin. The quarter moves the dime further because it has more momentum. Heavier objects have more momentum than lighter objects moving at the same speed. Tractor trailers have more momentum because they are heavier than cars.

Words to Know

cargo (KAR-goh)—goods that are carried from one place to another

diesel fuel (DEE-zuhl FYOO-uhl)—a heavy fuel that burns to make power; tractor trailers run on diesel fuel.

exhaust (eg-ZAWST)—the waste gases produced by the engine of a motor vehicle

kingpin (KING-pin)—a metal rod used to join a trailer to a tractor

log (LOG)—a written record; tractor trailer drivers keep a log of the time and distance of each trip.

Read More

Gentile, Petrina, Bobbie Kalman, and Marc Crabtree. *Big Trucks, Big Wheels.* Crabapples. New York: Crabtree Publishing, 1997.

Ready, Dee. *Trucks.* Mankato, Minn.: Bridgestone Books, 1998.

Stille, Darlene R. *Trucks.* A True Book. New York: Children's Press, 1997.

Internet Sites

American Trucking Associations
http://www.truckline.com
Ted and Trisha's Truck Stop
http://education.dot.gov/k5/truck.htm
Truckers.com
http://www.truckers.com

Index

L00005334

WARDLAW ELEMENTARY SCHOOL
1698 Oakwood Ave.
Vallejo, CA 94591
(707) 556-8730